DRAW WHAT SUCCESS LOOKS LIKE

THE COLORING AND ACTIVITY BOOK FOR SERIOUS BUSINESSPEOPLE

SARAH COOPER 😊 THECOOPERREVIEW.COM

Andrews McMeel Publishing®

a division of Andrews McMeel Universal

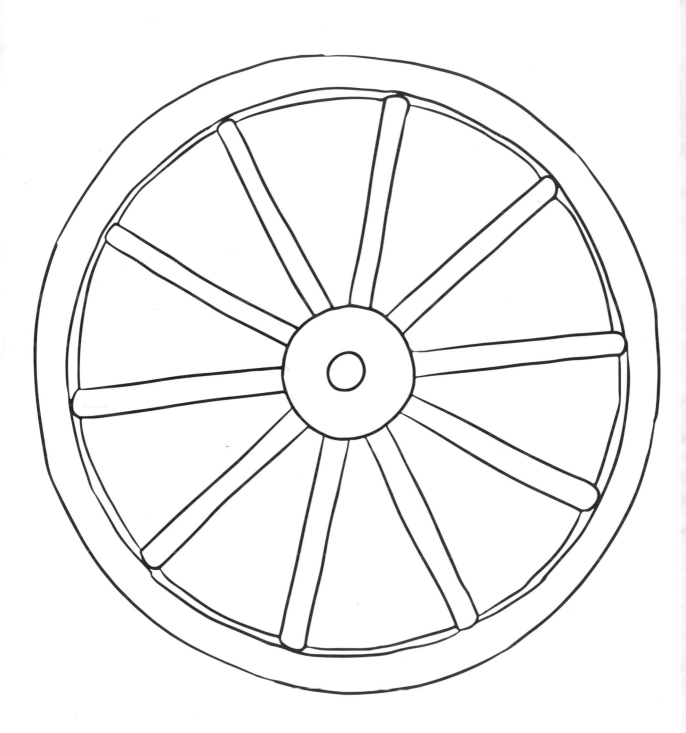

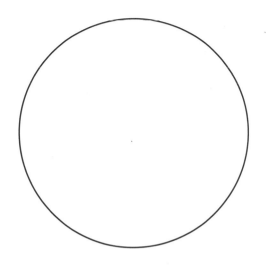
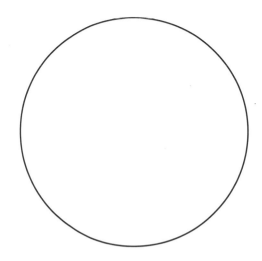

REINVENT THE WHEEL

SEE HOW MANY NEW AND INTERESTING WAYS YOU CAN DRAW A WHEEL. THIS WILL PREPARE YOU FOR THAT DAYLONG BRAINSTORMING MEETING COMING UP.

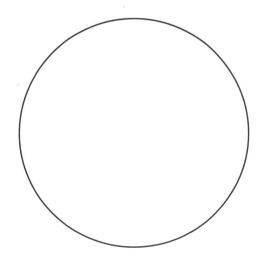
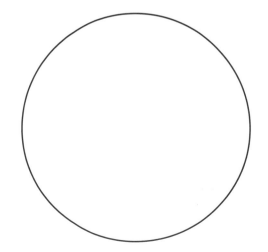

REAL-TIME feedback

IT'S ALWAYS A GOOD TIME TO GIVE FEEDBACK.

Use this real-time feedback tool to practice writing feedback for your coworkers.

eacR

TOOL

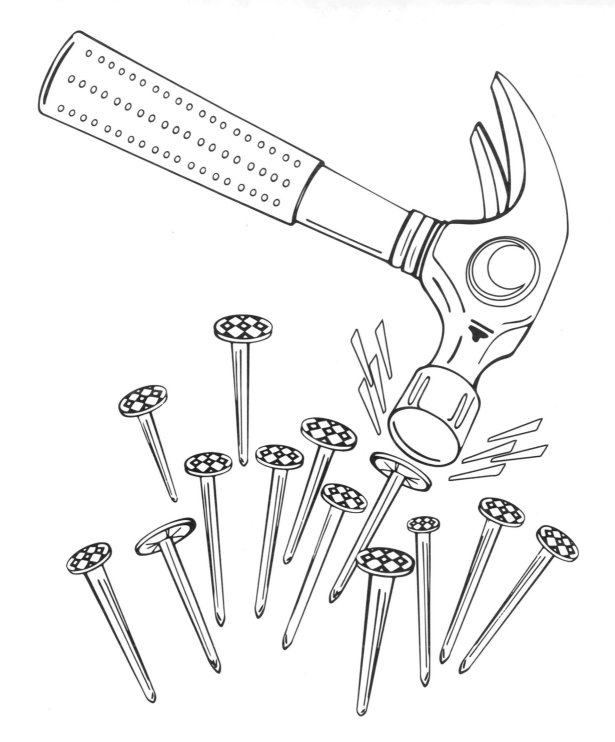

YOU HIT THE
NAIL ON THE HEAD

KEY METRICS TRACKER

KEEP TRACK OF WHENEVER ANYONE SAYS IT, INCLUDING YOURSELF.

CAN WE TAKE A STEP BACK HERE? _____

WHAT PROBLEM ARE WE TRYING TO SOLVE? _____

I SEE YOUR CONCERN _____

LET'S GET THE BALL ROLLING _____

LET'S TABLE THAT FOR NOW _____

CAN I JUMP IN HERE? _____

INTERESTING POINT _____

DO WE HAVE ANY DATA? _____

WILL THIS SCALE? _____

WHAT ARE THE TAKEAWAYS? _____

WHO CAN TAKE THIS ACTION ITEM? _____

WHAT ARE THE NEXT STEPS? _____

LET'S SCHEDULE A MEETING TO DISCUSS THAT _____

WHAT ARE THE BEST PRACTICES? _____

LET'S FOLLOW UP _____

LET'S DO A DEEP DIVE

TRY TO MAKE THIS B.H.A.G.

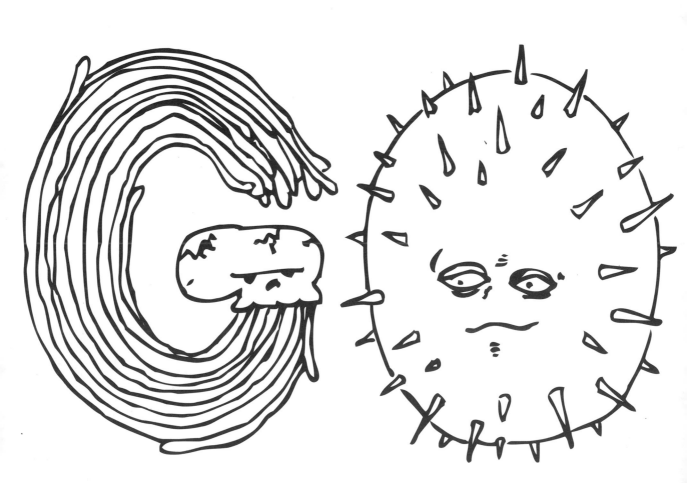

BIGGER & HAIRIER & SCARIER

RESIGNATION E-MAIL AD LIBS

Fellow _____,
_____ fun name for your team

It's with _____ that I must share with you my
_____ something sad, e.g., "a heavy heart"

decision to leave _____. This was a very difficult
_____ name of company

decision to make.

It's hard to believe that _____ ago, I was the _____.
_____ how long you've been there _____ your first position

From that time until when I was _____, and all the way
_____ your second position

to my current role as _____, I have grown so much. I've
_____ current position

learned so much, and hopefully taught all of you in return.

I am headed off to explore my next chapter _____

_____.
_____ the much more awesome thing you'll be doing

I'm excited about my future while I continue to be excited about

all the things you'll continue to accomplish here (except for you,

_____, you never finish anything)!
_____ person everyone
always makes fun of

If I could leave you all with just one thought, please remember

these words: _____.
_____ sage advice or Steve Jobs quote you found on Google

If you ever want to get in touch, my info is below.

This isn't good-bye; our paths will cross again. Hopefully at fare-well happy hour drinks at ___!
time

_____
your name

_____
phone number

_____
e-mail address

_____
blog

_____
LinkedIn

_____
Twitter

_____
Facebook

_____
Snapchat

_____
social media platform no one's ever heard of

WHAT'S ON YOUR RADAR?

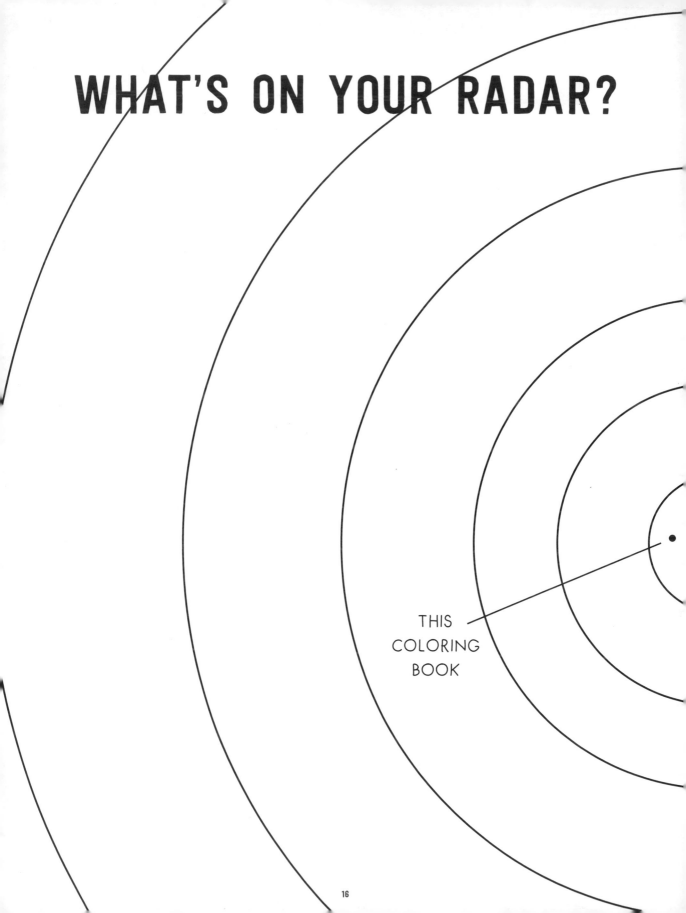

THIS
COLORING
BOOK

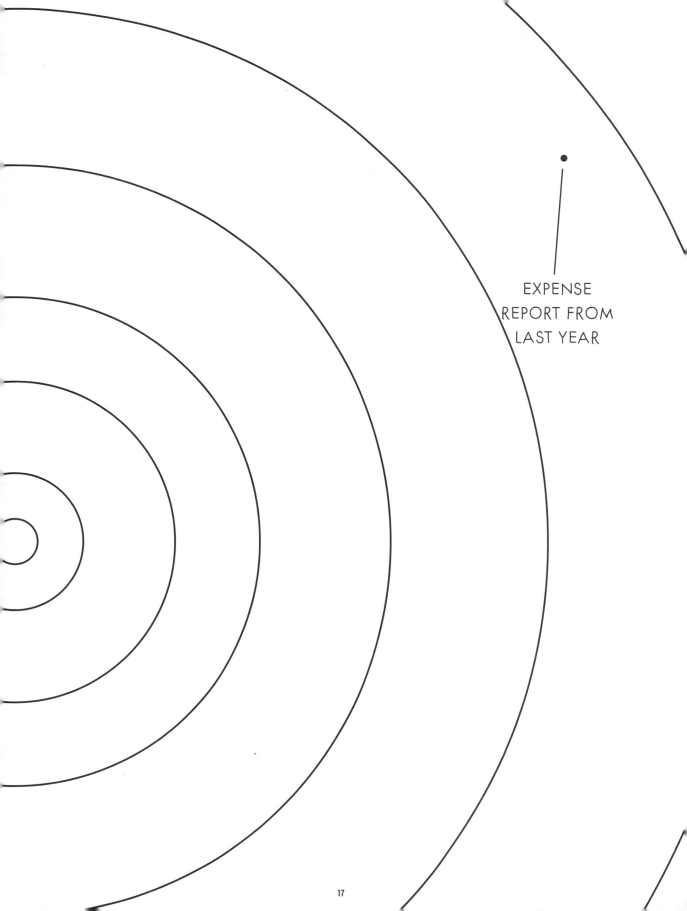

EXPENSE
REPORT FROM
LAST YEAR

NAME THE MOVIE

THESE FUN PHRASES CAME STRAIGHT FROM HOLLYWOOD
(WHO TOOK THEM STRAIGHT FROM SERIOUS BUSINESSPEOPLE).

"I DRINK YOUR MILK SHAKE" _____

"I COULD TELL YOU, BUT THEN I'D HAVE TO KILL YOU" _____

"ALWAYS BE CLOSING" _____

"DANGER IS MY MIDDLE NAME" _____

"WE'RE NOT IN KANSAS ANYMORE" _____

"I'M GONNA MAKE HIM AN OFFER HE CAN'T REFUSE" _____

"WHAT WE'VE GOT HERE IS FAILURE TO COMMUNICATE" _____

"YOU CAN'T HANDLE THE TRUTH" _____

"SHOW ME THE MONEY" _____

"ROUND UP THE USUAL SUSPECTS" _____

"I'LL BE BACK" _____

"HOUSTON, WE HAVE A PROBLEM" _____

"I'M THE KING OF THE WORLD!" _____

"KEEP YOUR FRIENDS CLOSE BUT YOUR ENEMIES CLOSER" _____

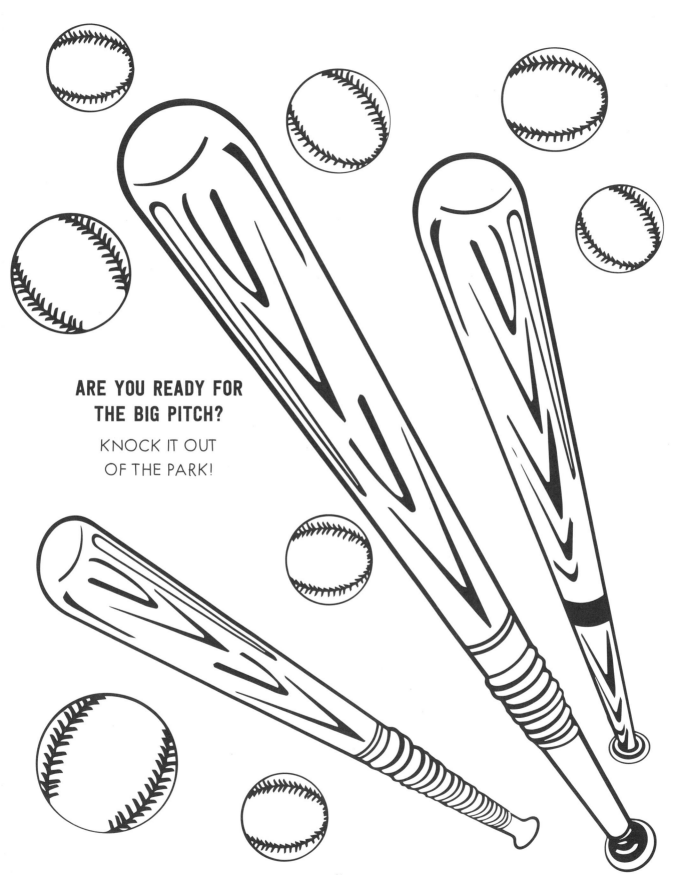

ARE YOU READY FOR
THE BIG PITCH?

KNOCK IT OUT
OF THE PARK!

EMERGENCY DISGUISE

EVERYONE'S DOING
A GREAT JOB

EXCEPT FOR:

_____

FLIP-FLOPPING

COLOR IN THE FLIP-FLOPS FOR A LITTLE THERAPEUTIC
RELEASE FROM INDECISIVE LEADERS.

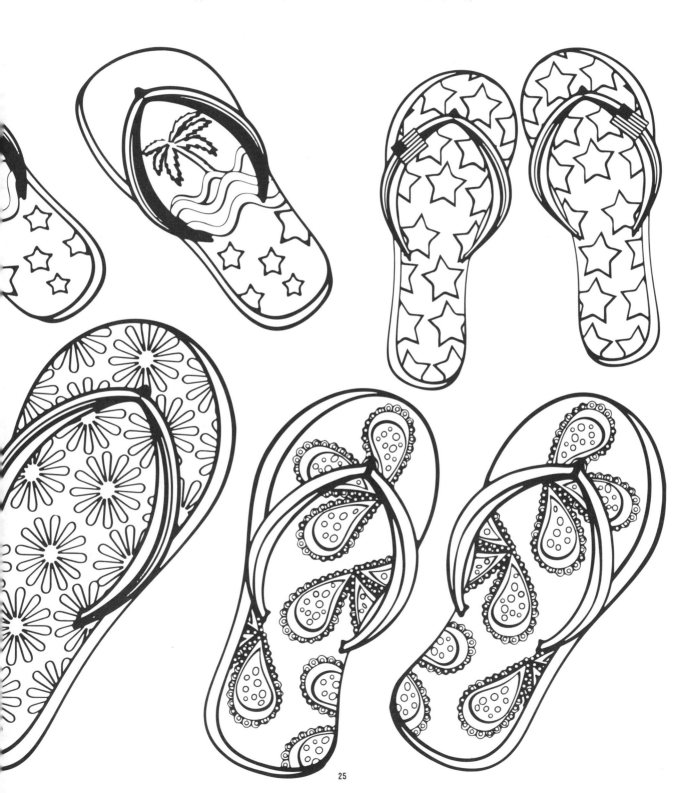

PEER REVIEW WORK SHEET

USE THIS WORK SHEET TO CONSTRUCT AS MANY SENTENCES AS
YOU NEED FOR YOUR PEER REVIEW MINIMUM WORD COUNT.

deep	passion	priorities
mediocre	grasp	consensus
arbitrary	handle	strategy
excellent	focus	how to execute
surprising	understanding	key insights
unnecessary	knowledge	big data
credible	mastery	useless details
pragmatic	acuity	team building
disappointing	perspicacity	mentoring
painful	ownership	deliverables
weird	approach	iteration
triumphant	orientation	design aesthetic
inspiring	cultivation	relationships
nebulous	expertise	vision

EXAMPLE:

Ben has a mediocre grasp of strategy. He has a
disappointing understanding of useless details.
Ben also has a painful focus on how to execute.

GET OUT OF YOUR COMFORT ZONE

COMFORT ZONE
↓

↓
PROMOTION

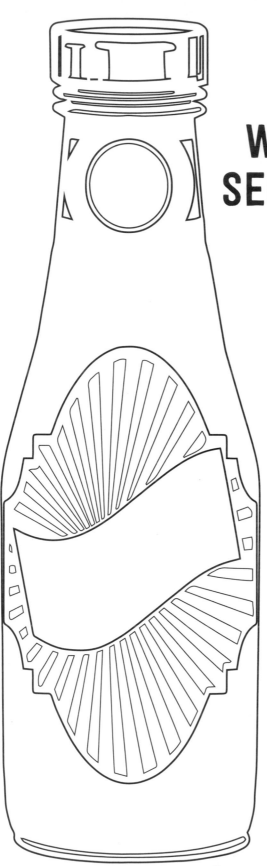

WHAT'S YOUR SECRET SAUCE?

Design your secret sauce bottle and list the ingredients (but don't let your competitors see!).

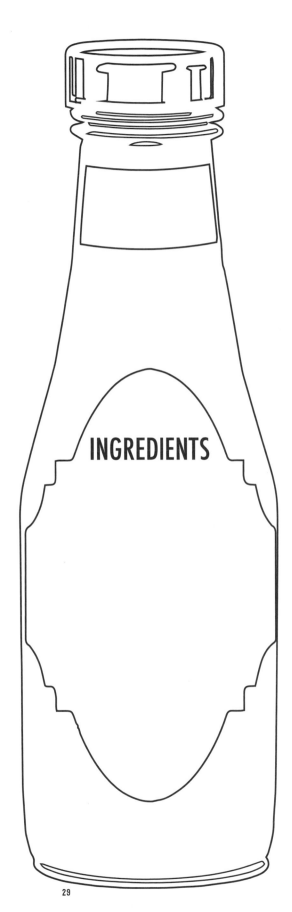

INGREDIENTS

It's OK to recycle
your ingredients
from other, more
successful products.

WHAT ARE THE TAKEAWAYS?

Pretend to write down the key takeaways here.

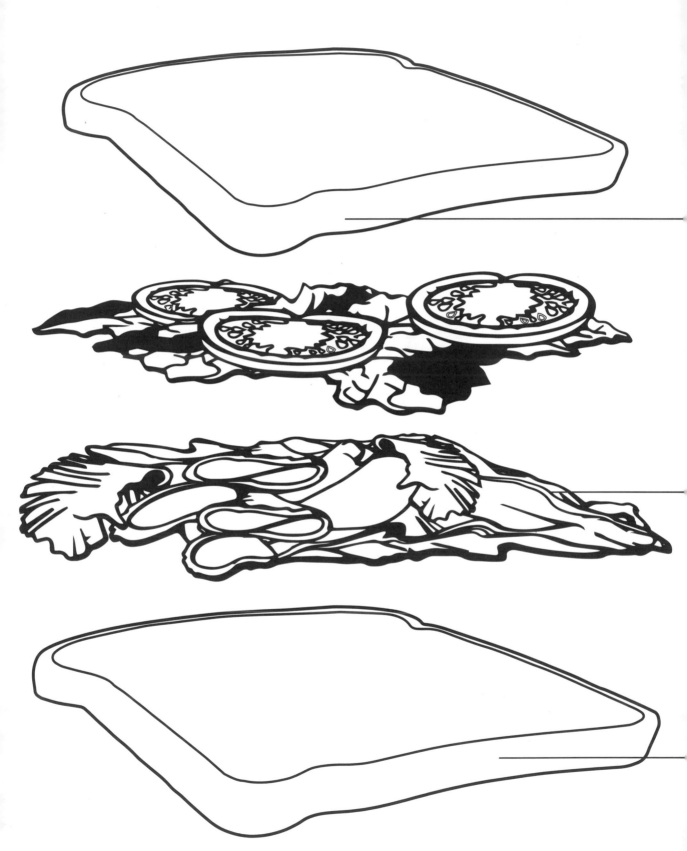

PRAISE SANDWICH WORK SHEET

Practice sandwiching your criticism between
two thin slices of compliments.

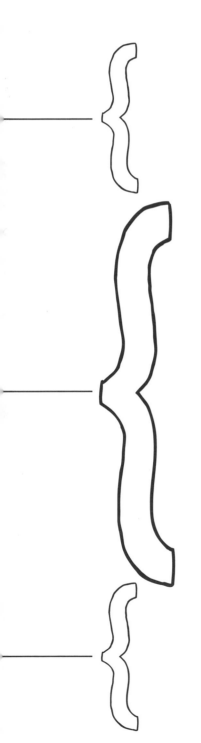

COMPLIMENTS

CRITICISM

COMPLIMENTS

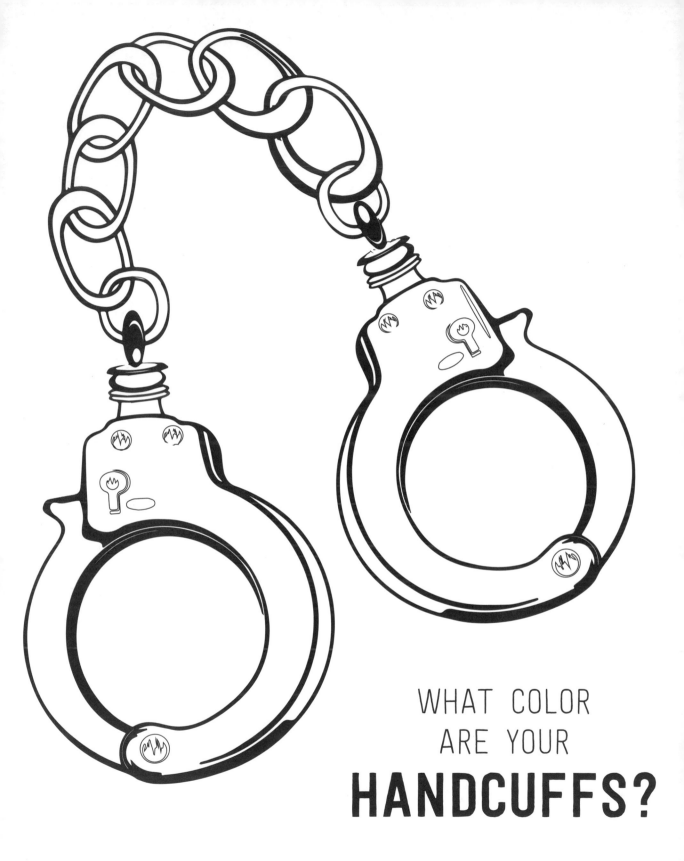

WHAT COLOR
ARE YOUR
HANDCUFFS?

YOUR STOCKS ARE VESTING!

Celebrate by coloring in these decorative vests.

CRUNCH THE NUMBERS

ANALYZE THE DATA

Plot the points to see how your product did this quarter.

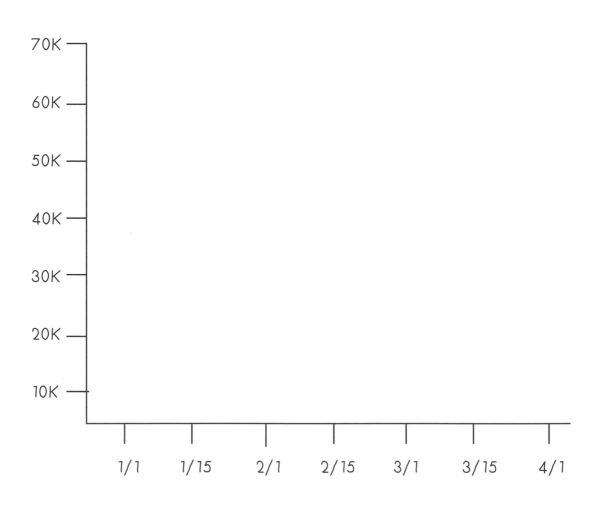

1/1: 69,450	3/1: 34,650
1/15: 64,054	3/15: 24,904
2/1: 59,493	4/1: 9,040
2/15: 43,078	

GOOD IDEA GRAVEYARD

RIP

RIP

RIP

RIP

RIP

RIP

Here lies
my idea for
Massage
Mondays.
Born: Dec. 3
Died: Dec. 3

RIP

RIP

WRITE DOWN ALL THE GREAT IDEAS YOU'VE HAD OVER
THE YEARS THAT WILL NEVER SEE THE LIGHT OF DAY.

DO YOU HAVE A BUSINESS MODEL?

Make your business model
as attractive as possible
before you meet with
potential investors.

MEETING OFFENDERS

This person uses the
meeting to catch up on
e-mail (or sleep)

Always says things like,
"I was just chatting
with the CEO"

Will say, "We can
get that done by
tomorrow, right?"

Always quick to
interrupt if he doesn't
like what he's hearing

EACH OFFICE HAS THEM. DRAW THE PROFILE OF
THE PERSON WHO BEST FITS THE PROFILE.

THE WHISPERER

Always in sidebar
conversations, and when
asked to speak up, says,
"Oh, nothing"

THE DUCKER

Will schedule a meeting,
show up, then leave
when he feels like it

THE TAPPER

Taps his feet, his
fingers, his pencil,
and/or sighs loudly

THE OVERTHANKER

Always thanking
everyone for everything

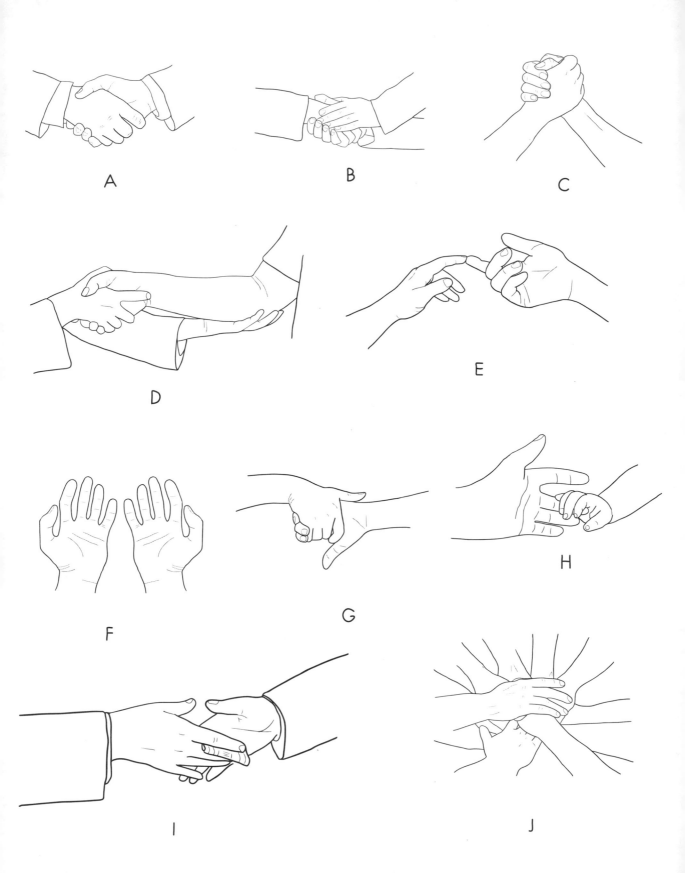

HANDSHAKE QUIZ

NAME A FEW SITUATIONS WHERE THIS GREETING MIGHT BE APPROPRIATE.

A   networking event, client meeting,

B   job interview,

C   poker night,

D   volunteering,

E   drunk mixer,

F   Broadway,

G   awkward good-bye,

H   boss's baby shower,

I   street corner,

J   team building event,

IS IT REPEATABLE?

Draw this exact same shape as many times as you can.

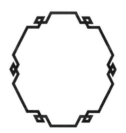

WILL IT SCALE?

Draw bigger and bigger triangles to see if it will scale.

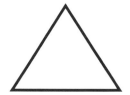

EMOTIONAL INTELLIGENCE QUIZ

_____   _____   _____

WHAT IS THE FACE SAYING?

WRITE DOWN THE EMOTION TO MATCH THE FACE.

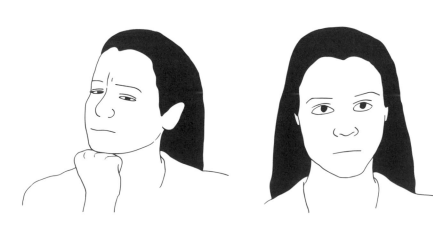

_____   _____   _____

"GREAT SPEECH, BOSS."

"OH, RIGHT! WE DID FORGET TO DOCUMENT THAT DECISION."

"IS ANYONE WRITING THIS DOWN?"

HOW DO YOU MAKE THAT FACE?

DRAW THE FACE TO MATCH THE EMOTION.

"HEY! IT'S ALMOST BEER:30!"

"WHO KEEPS SCHEDULING MEETINGS FOR 8 AM?"

"SORRY, MOUTH FULL."

WHAT DOES SUCCESS LOOK LIKE?

DRAW SUCCESS HERE.

WHAT DOES FAILURE LOOK LIKE?

DRAW FAILURE HERE.

MEETING SPEAK

MATCH THE COMMON MEETING PHRASE
TO WHAT IT REALLY MEANS.

This wasn't on my calendar	I'm pretty sure you're wrong
Duly noted	I need this to be over
Let's table that	I'll do the bare minimum
Can you repeat that?	Probably not
To your earlier point...	Let's keep talking about this forever
That said...	I have no idea what you're saying
It's a no-brainer	You will never hear from me again
Definitely	We are going to be here awhile
Can I ask a quick question?	Don't ever bring this up again
Happy to discuss this further	I'd like to change the subject
Let's streamline this process	I deleted this from my calendar
Sounds good to me	I've already forgotten about it
Let's get some data on that	I was looking at Facebook
I'll try my best	We're still not changing anything
Let's circle back later	I don't feel like thinking about it
I'll set a reminder to follow up	I'm kissing your ass
On a related note	That's the dumbest thing I've ever heard

WOULD YOU RATHER?

CIRCLE THE THING YOU'D RATHER DO THAN ATTEND THIS MEETING.

Walk on hot coals	Attend this meeting
Walk on glass	Attend this meeting
Walk 500 miles	Attend this meeting
Eat an ant	Attend this meeting
Skydive	Attend this meeting
Skydive without training	Attend this meeting
Skydive without a parachute	Attend this meeting
Have a root canal	Attend this meeting
Perform a root canal	Attend this meeting
Go to a Nickelback concert	Attend this meeting
Enter a clogging contest	Attend this meeting
Drink unpasteurized milk	Attend this meeting
Be on a reality TV show	Attend this meeting
Win then lose 1 billion dollars	Attend this meeting
Testify before Congress	Attend this meeting
Live in a cave	Attend this meeting

ARE YOU ADDING VALUE?

Add these values to show how much value you can add.

610 + 37	412 + 73	417 + 2	415 + 80	440 + 59
244 + 34	644 × 2	363 + 36	720 + 74	736 + 10
263 + 14	322 + 75	730 + 21	562 + 72	241 + 41
141 + 25	142 + 41	328 + 28	342 + 17	640 + 13
362 + 21	520 + 29	571 + 23	226 + 10	216 + 64

PRETEND TO TAKE NOTES

Write down every other word you hear, while nodding.
Circle or double-underline every so often.

_____

_____

_____

_____

_____

_____

_____

_____

_____

_____

_____

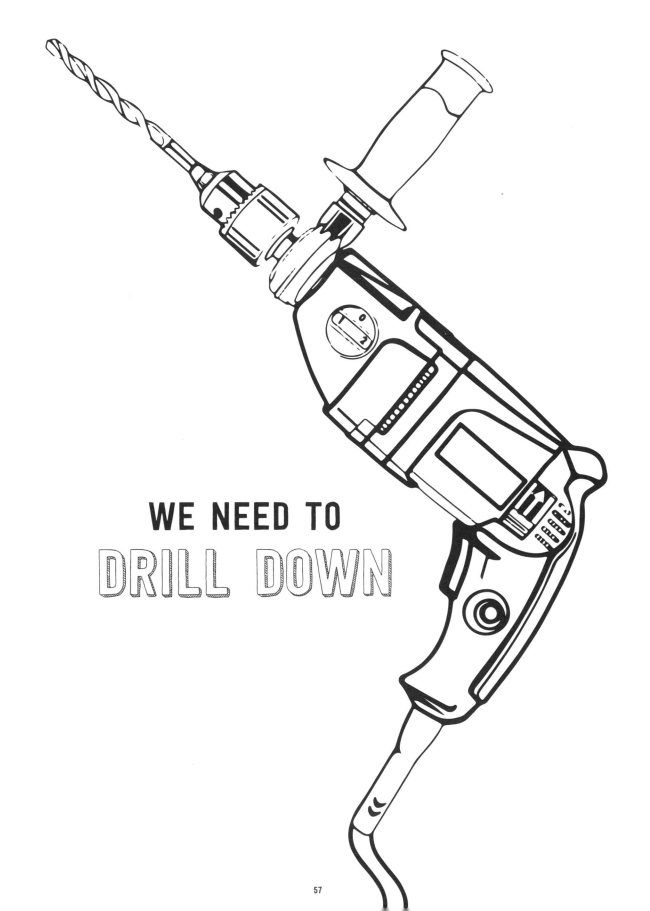

WE NEED TO
DRILL DOWN

DIVERSITY INITIATIVE

Our team isn't diverse enough! Use your drawing and coloring skills to create a truly diverse team.

THINK BIG

DRAW THE BIGGEST THINGS YOU CAN THINK OF.

BLUE SKY

Put your deepest thoughts in the clouds.

MANIFESTO AD LIBS

_____ ago, I enthusiastically joined _____. It has
how long ago you joined　　　　　　　　　　name of company

been a _____ experience. I proudly bleed _____
　　　　positive adjective　　　　　　　　　　　company colors

every day! I even have a temporary tattoo of the _____
　　　　　　　　　　　　　　　　　　　　　name of company logo

on the back of my leg.

But all is not _____. _____ recently wrote an
　　　　　positive noun　　news publication

article about us, detailing our terrible record on _____.
　　　　　　　　　　　　　　　　　　　　what your company has
a terrible record on

I wanted to share what I think is _____ and recommend a
　　　　　　　　　　　　　　negative adjective

path forward.

Our Three Problems

1. We lack a focused, cohesive _____.
　　　　　　　　　　　　　　　　the thing your company lacks

We've known this for _____, but have done nothing about it. I've
　　　　　　　vague amount of time

heard our _____ described as _____.
　　　　noun　　　　　　food metaphor for bad strategy

I hate _____. We all should.
　food from previous metaphor

2. We don't have clear _____.
　　　　　　　　　　　thing that's not clear

The most painful manifestation of this is the massive _____
　　　　　　　　　　　　　　　　　　　　　big problem with
your company

that exists throughout the organization. There's a reason

why _____. We're not doing that.
　sports metaphor about
how to win a game

3. We lack _____.

the other thing your company lacks

Combine _____ with _____, and the result is

first problem   second problem

_____.

third problem

Solving Our Problems

1. Focus on _____.

what your company should focus on

We need to get rid of _____ and eliminate _____.

first thing to get rid of   second thing to get rid of

2. Restore _____.

what your company should restore

By building around a strong _____ structure, we will

jargon

eliminate significant _____.

what you'll eliminate

3. Blow up the _____ and kill the _____.

what needs to be blown up (figuratively)   what needs to be killed (figuratively)

Empower a new model of _____. Align a set

some model you read in a business book

of _____ so that they are not _____.

important sounding nouns   the thing they shouldn't be doing

This won't be easy. It will take _____. I very much

positive nouns, e.g., "tenacity"

look forward to the challenge. Let's _____ and stop

thing to do from the earlier sports metaphor

eating _____.

the bad thing from the earlier food metaphor

HOW SOON UNTIL YOU BURN OUT?

I was last on the
To: line in an
e-mail from my
boss to the team

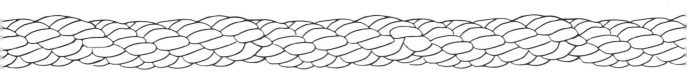

WHEN SOMETHING STRESSFUL HAPPENS, ADD IT HERE.
THEN YOU CAN COUNT DOWN THE DAYS UNTIL
YOU REACH THE END OF YOUR ROPE.

INTERVIEW QUESTIONS TRACKER

Keep track of whenever you ask it.

WHY DO YOU WANT TO WORK HERE? _____

WHAT ARE YOUR STRENGTHS? _____

WHAT ARE YOUR WEAKNESSES? _____

HOW WOULD YOU FIND
YOUR WAY OUT OF A PICKLE? _____

IF YOU WERE ME, WOULD YOU HIRE YOU? _____

IF I WERE YOU, WOULD YOU
WANT ME TO HIRE ME? _____

HOW OLD ARE YOU? UH, I MEAN,
WHAT YEAR DID YOU GRADUATE? _____

WHAT DO YOU LIKE TO DO FOR FUN? _____

WHAT IS THE BIGGEST CHALLENGE
YOU'VE EVER FACED? _____

TELL ME ABOUT A TIME WHEN YOU LOST
YOUR KEYS. HOW DID YOU FIND THEM? _____

CAN YOU HELP ME FIX MY WEBSITE? _____

HOW DO YOU FEEL ABOUT TABLE TENNIS? _____

MAKE AN IMPACT

HIT THIS PAGE AS HARD AS YOU CAN

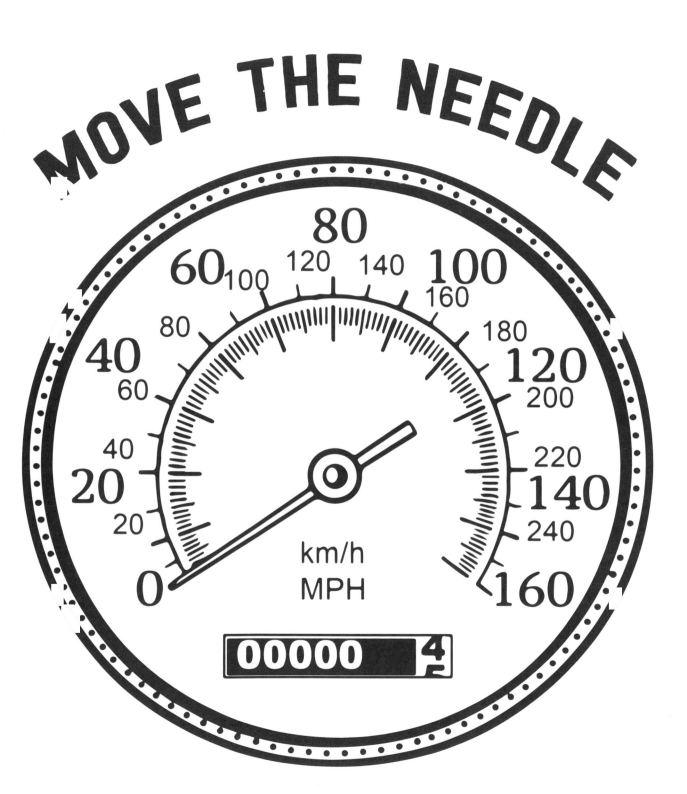

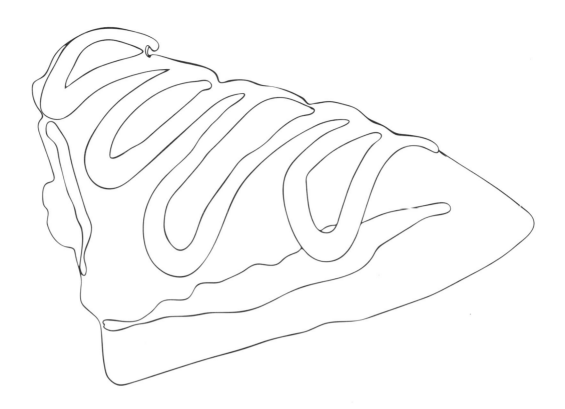

REDUCE TURNOVER

Draw a smaller version of this delicious apple turnover.

COWORKER CARD WORK SHEET

Happy
Birthday!

Feel
Better!

Practice what you're going to write in your coworker's card before you go screwing it up in the real thing.

Welcome Back!

Sorry to See You Go!

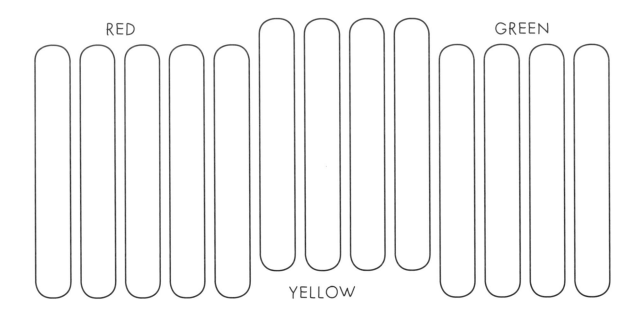

RED

GREEN

YELLOW

CHANGE YOUR TONE

SOMEONE DOESN'T LIKE YOUR TONE?
PRACTICE CHANGING YOUR TONE BY COLORING
DIFFERENT SHADES HERE.

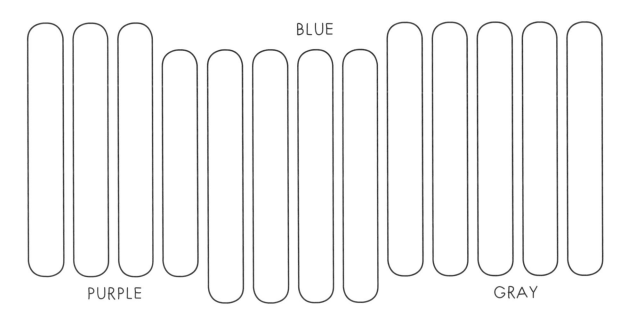

BLUE

PURPLE

GRAY

GET ON THE SAME PAGE

Get all of your coworkers to look at this page at the same time.
This will be a huge accomplishment.

KICKOFF MEETING

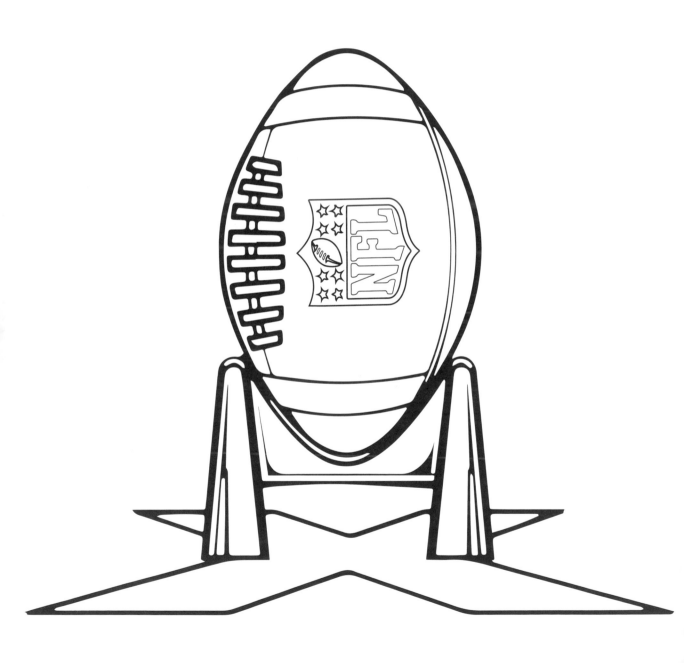

MEETING HALL OF FAME

Keep track of all the types of meetings you've been to.
You get a prize for each one. But not really.

KICKOFF MEETING _____

FOLLOW-UP MEETING _____

TEAM UPDATE _____

BRAINSTORMING MEETING _____

1-ON-1 WITH MY MANAGER _____

1-ON-1 WITH MY DIRECT REPORT _____

1-ON-1 WITH MY INTERN _____

SKIP LEVEL 1-ON-1 _____

PAINFUL NETWORKING EVENT _____

3-HOUR CONFERENCE CALL _____

VIDEO CONFERENCE CALL _____

NO IDEA WHY WE'RE MEETING _____

BRAIN DUMP AFTER BEING FIRED _____

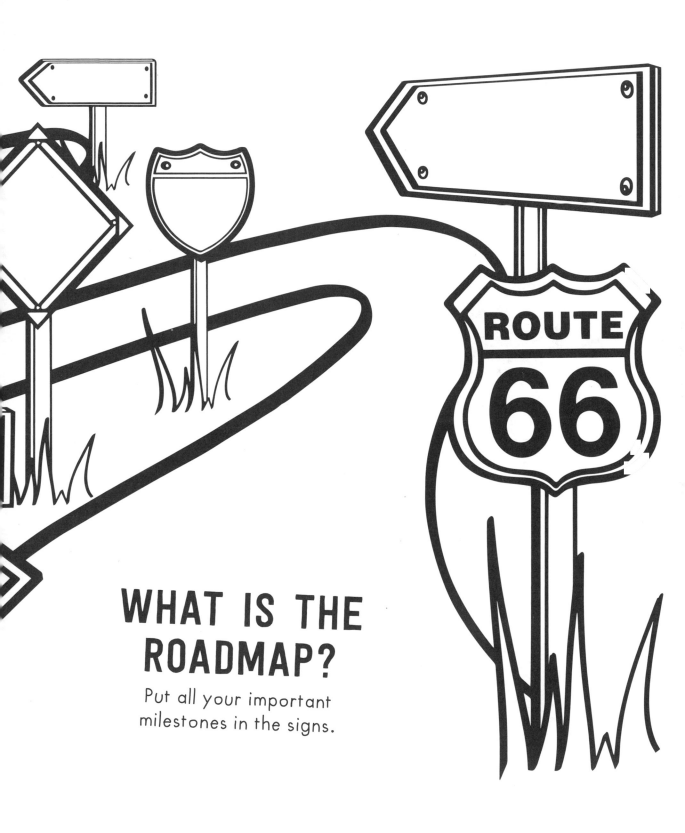

WHAT IS THE ROADMAP?

Put all your important milestones in the signs.

BUILD YOUR
STRAW MAN

BEST OF BREED

Draw your best-of-breed solutions.

GET ALL
YOUR DUCKS
IN A ROW

WHAT'S ON YOUR PLATE?

EXIT STRATEGY

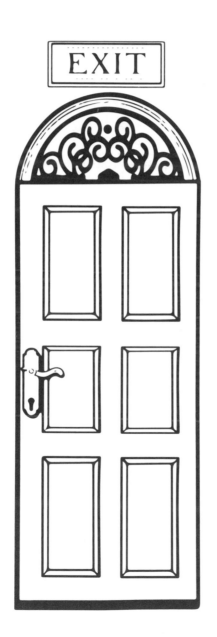

You have multiple exits! Pick your favorite one and color it.

COMPANY CULTURE

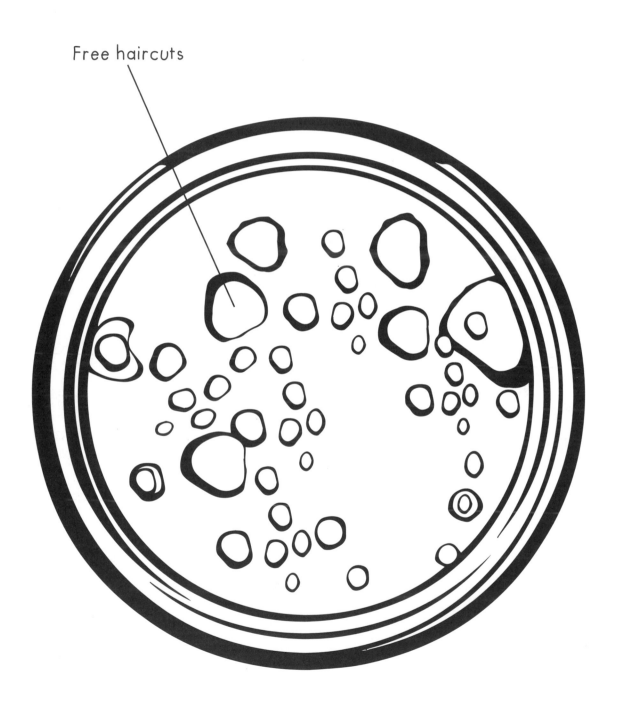

Free haircuts

YOUR COMPANY'S CULTURE IS VERY IMPORTANT.
CREATE A CULTURE YOU'D BE PROUD OF AND
NEVER EVER WANT TO LEAVE.

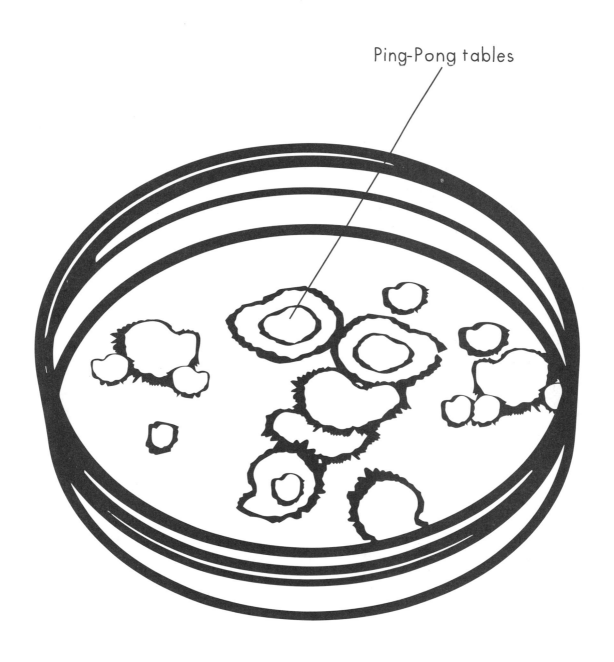

Ping-Pong tables

ESCALATOR

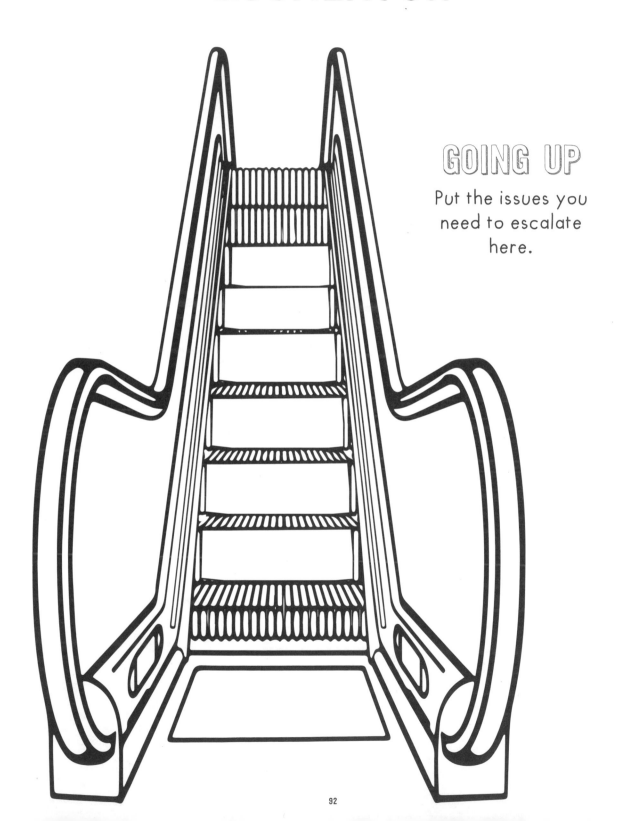

GOING UP

Put the issues you need to escalate here.

DE-ESCALATOR

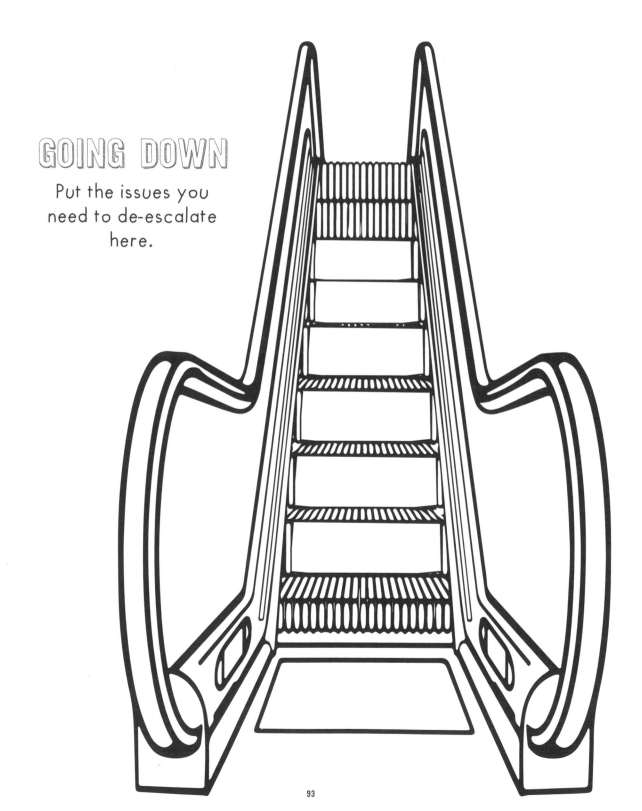

GOING DOWN

Put the issues you need to de-escalate here.

WHAT DO YOU BRING
TO THE TABLE?

Draw everything you bring to the table so that a potential employer can see all the reasons to hire you.

FOCUS ON
EXECUTING

BLEEDING-EDGE
TECHNOLOGY

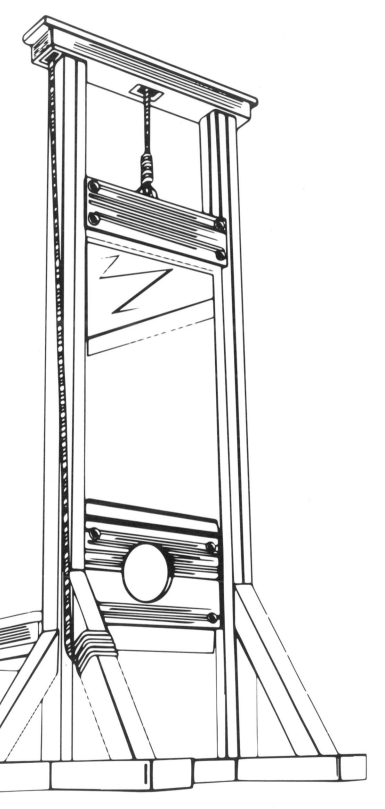

I DON'T SEE ANY
RED FLAGS.

DRAW SOME RED FLAGS HERE.

ARE YOU LASER-FOCUSED?

OUTLINE AND COLOR THE LASERS
SO THEY'RE MORE FOCUSED, LIKE YOU ARE.

FIRE ON ALL CYLINDERS

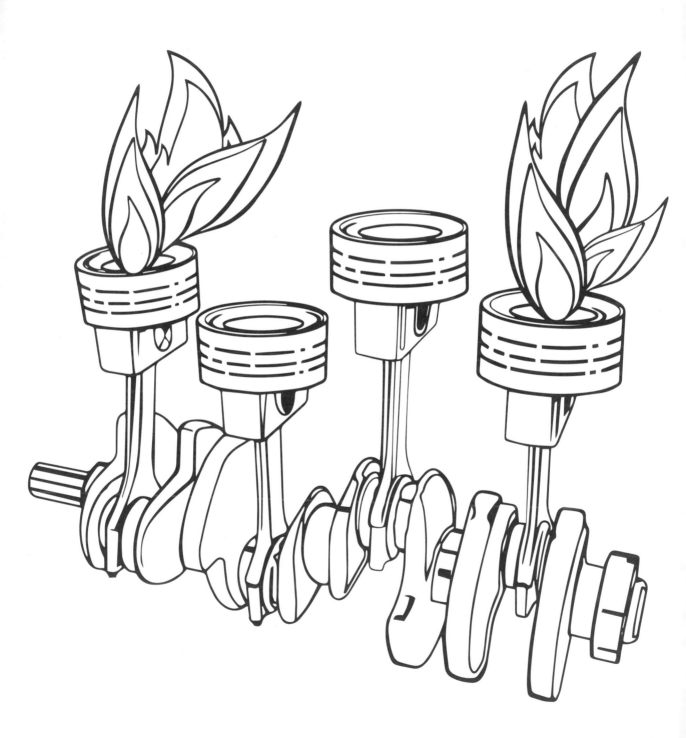

Not all cylinders are firing! Draw a fire in all cylinders.

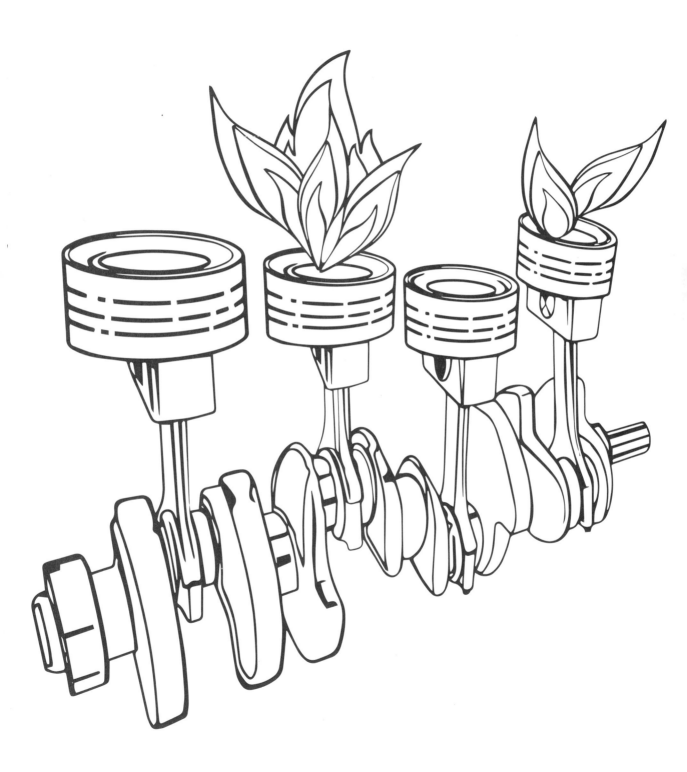

UNCANNY VALLEY

UH-OH. WE'VE REACHED AN UNCANNY VALLEY.
MAKE THE VALLEYS MORE SIMILAR, OR MORE DIFFERENT.

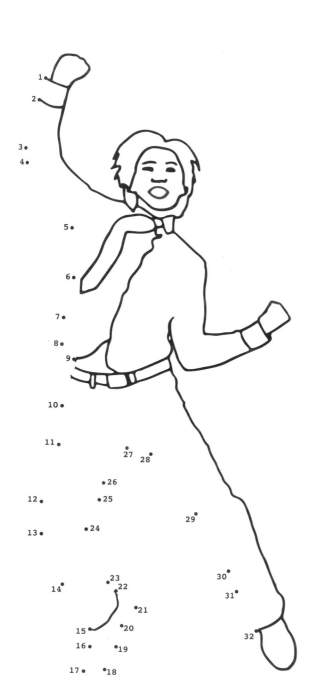

LET'S CONNECT THE DOTS

DEVIL'S ADVOCATE PRACTICE

Write down the opposite of each statement to
practice playing devil's advocate.

WE DON'T NEED DATA   But what if... _____

IT'S GOOD ENOUGH   But what if... _____

WE CAN DO IT LATER   But what if... _____

THIS IS A GREAT IDEA   But what if... _____

LET'S SHARE THIS
WITH THE TEAM   But what if... _____

OUR CUSTOMERS WON'T
NOTICE THAT   But what if... _____

YOU CAN HANDLE THIS
ON YOUR OWN   But what if... _____

OUR CLIENTS NEED THIS   But what if... _____

THIS PROJECT WAS SUCCESSFUL   But what if... _____

WE CAN DO IT BETTER   But what if... _____

LET'S COME UP WITH
A NEW STRATEGY   But what if... _____

LET'S FIX THE
UNDERLYING PROBLEM   But what if... _____

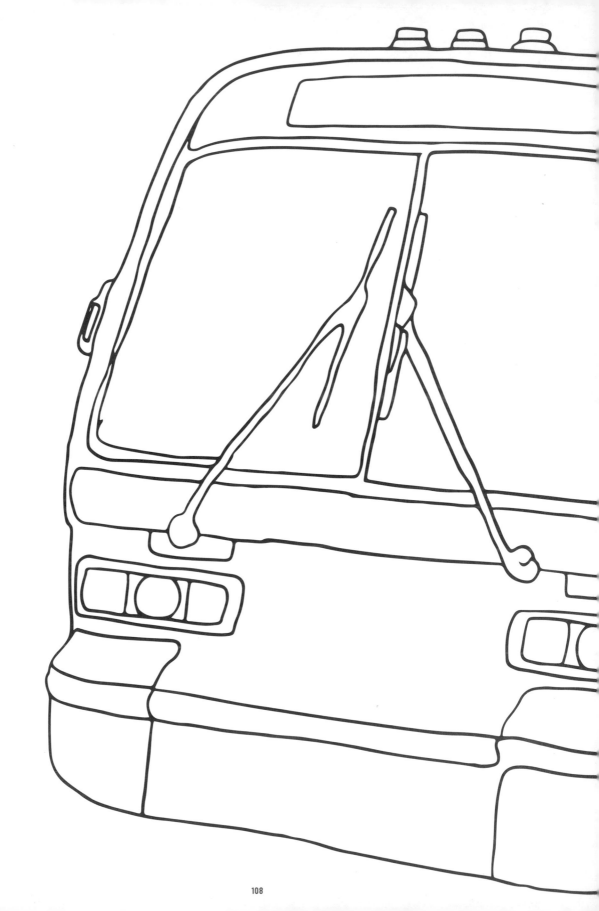

MEETING SURVIVAL KIT

WORK-LIFE BALANCE

Your work-life balance is all out of whack.
Add a few things to the life side
to even it out again.

WHAT IS OUR BENCHMARK?

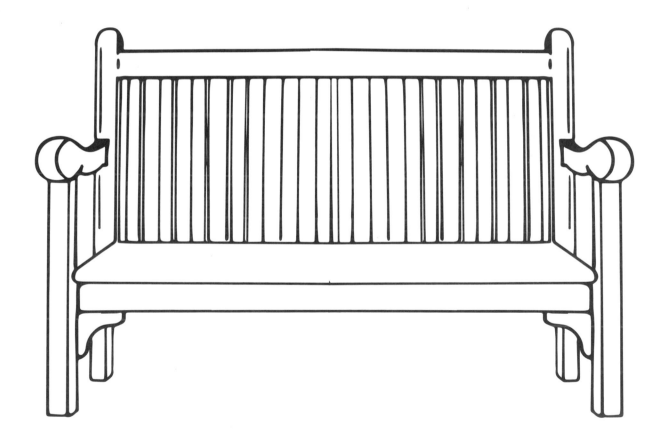

DRAW A MARK SITTING ON THIS BENCH.

WHO'S DRIVING THIS?

Right now, no one is.
Draw someone driving this before the whole project crashes.

LOW-
HANGING
FRUIT

ACTION FIGURES

TIME
TO
PIVOT

POSTMORTEM AD LIBS

Team,

This has been an incredible _____. We've had some high points,
                              _{time period}

such as _____, and some low points, such as _____.
        _{thing that went well}   _{thing that didn't go well}

I want to talk to you more about _____ to see where we went
                                 _{thing that didn't go well}

wrong and what we can do better next time.

First, the team we assembled was _____, but there was
                                 _{positive adjective}

no clear _____. This should have been fixed immediately.
         _{something that was missing}

_____ and I have taken responsibility for that, but obviously
_{employee name}

the responsibility lies with all of us.

Second, our _____ started out strong but then became
            _{noun, pural}

really _____. What went wrong there? I am _____
       _{negative adjective}   _{adjective}

to hear your thoughts.

Finally, right in the middle of the project, _____. This was
                                             _{unexpected thing that happened}

completely unavoidable by all accounts.

Thank you, everyone, for your _____ work on this. I know
                              _{positive adjective}

it will go better next time.

WHAT ARE YOUR NEXT STEPS?

Andrews McMeel Publishing
a division of Andrews McMeel Universal
1130 Walnut Street, Kansas City, Missouri 64106

www.andrewsmcmeel.com

16 17 18 19 20 MLY 10 9 8 7 6 5 4 3 2 1

ISBN: 978-1-4494-7606-9

Additional illustrations by Dawn Larder

Editor: Patty Rice
Designer, Art Director: Diane Marsh
Production Manager: Cliff Koehler
Production Editor: Erika Kuster

ATTENTION: SCHOOLS AND BUSINESSES
Andrews McMeel books are available at quantity discounts with bulk purchase for
educational, business, or sales promotional use. For information, please e-mail the
Andrews McMeel Publishing Special Sales Department: specialsales@amuniversal.com.